My Body Is Growing

A Guide for Children, Ages 4 to 8

Written and Illustrated by
Dagmar Geisler

Translated by
Andrea Jones Berasaluce

Sky Pony Press
New York

Sky Pony Press books may be purchased in bulk at special discounts for sales promotion, corporate gifts, fund-raising, or educational purposes. Special editions can also be created to specifications. For details, contact the Special Sales Department, Sky Pony Press, 307 West 36th Street, 11th Floor, New York, NY 10018 or info@skyhorsepublishing.com.

Sky Pony® is a registered trademark of Skyhorse Publishing, Inc.®, a Delaware corporation.
Visit our website at www.skyponypress.com.

10 9 8 7 6 5 4 3 2 1

Manufactured in China, March 2020
This product conforms to CPSIA 2008

Library of Congress Cataloging-in-Publication Data is available on file.

Cover design by Daniel Brount
Cover illustration by Dagmar Geisler

Print ISBN: 978-1-5107-4659-6
Ebook ISBN: 978-1-5107-4670-1

Table of Contents

6   Class 4b

14   Boys Scuffle, Girls Hold Hands—Is That True?

16   Good or Bad? Right or Wrong?

18   Saying Yes, Saying No—It's Not That Easy!

20   Yes or No! How Does It Feel?

22   Saying No Is Sometimes Quite Difficult!

26   Children Have Rights

28   Equal Rights for Girls and Boys. Yes, Of Course!

30   Firewoman, Pediatric Nurse— What Do I Want to Be?

32   Full Coverage— Older Siblings in Puberty

34   Puberty—Not Everything Is on the Outside

36   And What's Up With Love?

38   Help! I'm Going to Be an Uncle!

40   So, Here's How It Goes!

42   You Can Always Fall In Love

45   Resources

48   Index

Girls cry easily!

BOYS ARE COOL!

Boys never cry!

boys WRITE LiKE CHICKEN scratch!

GIRLS are bad AT MATH!

Boys are LOUD!

GIRLS ARE PRISSY!

BOYS PLAY WITH COMPUTERS!

GIRLS LOVE BARBIES!

all girls rock pink!

Boys Love cars!

GIRLS ARE NEAT!

BOYS ARE MESSY!

Boys don't like to bathe!

Girls are always giggling!

Girls are QUIEt!

Boys always tussle!

Girls like to Read

Girls love HorsEs!

BOYS are STRONG!

Class 4b

In Class 4B, there are 25 children: 12 girls and 13 boys. Some things about them we can see from the outside.

Stella has red hair.

Toby wears glasses.

Nicki is the tallest.

Jasper has curls.

Pauline has freckles.

Radley is blond.

Robert is dark-haired.

Pia usually wears a red sweater.

Lisa has green eyes.

Bernard is the smallest in the class.

Luis is tall and thin.

Hannah has long blond hair.

Hazima has a ponytail.

Lance always has the most fashionable clothes.

Paul always wears a hat.

Sam has braces.

Kurt is the huskiest.

Dale has broad shoulders.

Regina is small and thin.

Uriel has bristly brown hair.

Kai has brown eyes.

Serafina has long curls.

Daniel wears a size 7 shoe.

Lea recently got glasses.

David is missing an incisor.

But there's a lot you can't see from the outside.

Stella does judo.

Toby can whistle through the gap in his teeth.

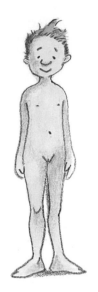

Nicki loves horses.

Jasper plays violin.

Pauline knows a hundred poems by heart.

Radley wants to be an astronaut.

Robert collects mini teddy bears and plush dinosaurs.

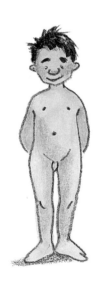

Pia can ride a unicycle.

Lisa can juggle five balls.

Bernard is on the swim team.

Luis wants to be a ballet dancer.

Hannah is the best at math.

Hazima is in Chess Club.

Lance knits.

Paul is also in Chess Club.

Sam is in Drama Club.

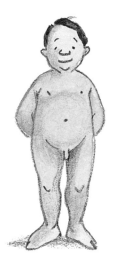

Kurt boxes.

Dale can draw beautifully.

Regina wants to be a painter.

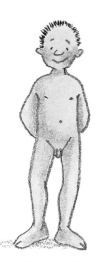

Uriel writes poems.

Kai is the class president.

Serafina can skateboard.

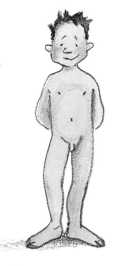

Daniel is the best at Language Arts.

Lea plays handball.

David is on the soccer team.

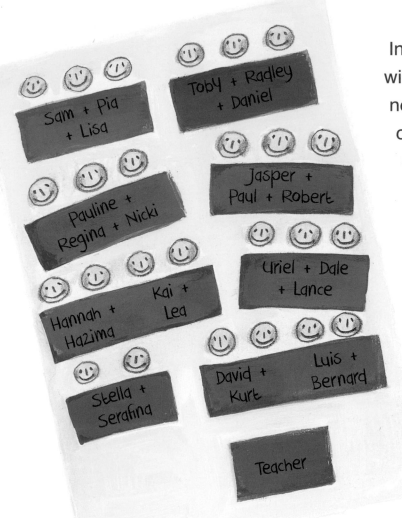

In Class 4B, all the girls sit by the window. Stella sits at the very front, next to Serafina. They are the best of friends. At the very back sit Sam, Pia, and Lisa. The three of them are always giggling. Hannah, Hazima, Kai, and Lea sit in the second row. Kai is the class president and Lea is the vice president. Pauline, Regina, and Nicki sit in the third row and like to write each other little notes.

On the other side, by the door, sit the boys. Toby, Radley, and Daniel sit at the very back. They goof around a lot, and so they are often separated from each other by the teacher. But by the next morning, they usually are sitting together again. Jasper, Paul, and Robert have their seats in the third row. In the very front sit David and Kurt, Luis and Bernard, and behind them are Uriel, Dale, and Lance. Dale always doodles little figures on his note paper. Uriel often daydreams. "Uriel's head is in the clouds again," the teacher says.

Back in first grade, Jasper sat next to Sam. Jasper and Sam were even in Ms. Lichtenberg's toddler group together. Jasper was Sam's best friend. Every morning Sam met up with him and they went to school together.

Jasper + Sam

But ever since last year, every time Sam goes by Jasper's house, he is always away. Sam now meets up first with Pia, then with Lisa, and goes to school along Garden Street. If Jasper comes across Sam in the school-yard, he looks away quickly. Nevertheless, David, Robert, and the other boys yell out, "Jasper and Sam are in love!" when Sam appears with her friends.

"Not true at all!" Jasper then screams. He gets really angry.

When Toby sees how Serafina rounds the corner on her skateboard, he feels like there's a butterfly caught in his stomach. It feels good, but also somehow stupid. When Serafina goes by him, Toby pulls her hair and says, "Stupid cow!" and "Sissy" to her. Sometimes Toby imagines himself marrying Serafina when he grows up. This he tells only to his old teddy bear, Hubert, in the evening when nobody else is around.

Serafina thinks Toby is nice when he smiles and whistles through the gap in his teeth. Once, when no one was looking, he gave her a cookie. But when he's mean, he gets on her nerves. "Get yourself dentures, you stupid gap-toothed twit!" she yells then and speeds off on her skateboard. Or she walks arm-in-arm with Stella around the schoolyard, and then jostles Toby and sticks her tongue out at him.

"I'm never going to fall in love," Toby says to his friends. "Girls are so stupid."

"Exactly," the others agree. Only Hubert could say otherwise, but nobody asks him.

Serafina likes Toby, but he annoys her. Toby likes Serafina, but he pulls her hair and yells insults at her.

"Of course," Serafina's mother says. "He teases you because he likes you! If boys and girls quarrel, then they like each other. Clear as day!"

Is that true?

When Kurt runs into Stella, he often kicks her shin or pinches her arm. Kurt cannot stand Stella. No butterflies fly in his stomach. He simply finds Stella stupid. And Stella thinks Kurt is stupid. And how! Stella never talks to Kurt. Never ever! Not even on the class trip, when the two of them accidentally had to sit next to each other on the bus.

"Kurt is in lo-oo-ve" the other boys sometimes shout. But Kurt is not in love, really he isn't. At least not with Stella.

Boys Scuffle, Girls Hold Hands— Is That True?

Pauline is friends with Regina and Nicki. In the schoolyard, the three of them usually walk arm-in-arm in a long row. Pauline is a little bit better friends with Regina. Sometimes the two of them walk around and hold hands. This gives Pauline a nice warm feeling.

   Radley is friends with Daniel. When Daniel comes around the corner in the morning, Radley is happy. "Hey Dan!" he shouts and jabs his friend in the ribs. "Hey Radley, you punk!" yells Daniel and he claps Radley on the back. Sometimes the two then begin to scuffle and roll around on the ground together.

Scuffling isn't so bad. Much worse is not having anyone to play with.

Jasper is Paul's best friend. When Paul sees Jasper, he claps him on the back. Jasper doesn't really like this. He would prefer to take Paul by the hand. But he punches him in the side instead.

Good or Bad? Right or Wrong?

Roughhousing is good:
When Radley and Daniel scuffle with each other, it's good for them.

Roughhousing is bad:
When Kurt scuffles with Stella, he hurts her. Stella doesn't like that. Luis, Lance, Robert, Jasper, and Uriel don't like rough-housing either. Jasper even gets really nervous, since he once broke his arm in a scuffle. For a whole month he couldn't play the violin.

Holding hands is good:
Pauline and Regina like to walk hand-in-hand. Jasper would really love to walk hand-in-hand with Paul but doesn't dare.

Holding hands is bad:
When Mama picks up Lea from school, she some-times takes Lea by the hand. Then Lea feels em-barrassed.

Cuddling is nice:

For Robert there is nothing nicer than snuggling up at home with his dad. Dad always smells so good. Sitting with Dad on the couch, Robert is as happy as a clam.

Cuddling is terrible:

When Aunt Olga comes to visit, Nicki makes herself scarce. Aunt Olga always holds Nicki so tight that she can barely breathe. Each time she gives Nicki a slobbery kiss on the cheek. It always leaves a smudge of pink lipstick behind. Also, Aunt Olga's perfume smells like lilies of the valley. Whoa!

Good, bad! Nice, terrible! Is it right or wrong?

Very easy. What you find nice is good. What you don't is bad!

And if one person finds it nice and another doesn't?

It has to be nice for everyone, otherwise it doesn't work!

Saying Yes, Saying No –
It's Not That Easy!

I don't have to scuffle!

I can let someone take me into his/ her arms, even if it makes others giggle!

I don't have to be kissed if I don't want to be!

If I don't want to be hugged, I can say NO!

In my room, I can be all alone!

If I'm in the bathroom and Mama wants desperately to come in too, I can say NO!

If Aunt Babette wants to kiss me, I can say YES! I really love Aunt Babette. She always smells so good. When Uncle Theo sees how I kiss Aunt Babette, he also wants a kiss. I don't want to kiss Uncle Theo. He always laughs so loudly and has a scratchy beard. I can say NO! to Uncle Theo. Even if Uncle Theo doesn't understand why Aunt Babette gets a kiss and he doesn't.

I can have a secret with my best friend and don't need to tell, even if everyone asks me. I say NO!

Yes or No!
How Does It Feel?

When I snuggle with Papa, my stomach feels very warm, as if it were full of warm vanilla pudding. (Robert)

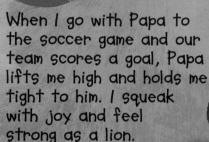

When Grandma hugs me, I feel like I'm lying on a soft cloud. She smells like rose soap and freshly baked cakes. (Sam)

When I go with Papa to the soccer game and our team scores a goal, Papa lifts me high and holds me tight to him. I squeak with joy and feel strong as a lion. (David)

YES!

Sometimes Mama gives me small kisses on the back of my neck, then tickles my skin, as if a thousand ladybugs were walking over it. Especially along my back. (Jasper)

Grandpa smells of pipe tobacco and usually has on a thick, scratchy wool jacket. When he takes me in his arms, I get the feeling that nothing bad can happen to me. (Regina)

My friend and I have a secret. It belongs only to us. We don't tell it to anyone. When I think about it, I become very tingly with pleasure. (Lisa)

When Aunt Babette caresses my cheek, it feels like a butterfly touched me. Her hand is quite cool and smooth and soft. (Lea)

20

Aunt Olga's slobbery kisses feel disgusting. As if a snail were slithering over my cheek. Afterward, I always have to wipe off the lipstick. Whoa! (Nicki)

When Dad takes me in his arms, sometimes he lifts me up like a baby. I find it stupid. (Bernard)

When Uncle Thorsten comes to visit, he hugs me so hard that it hurts. I don't like that. (Stella)

My friend's older brother is so cool. But when no one's looking, he tries to give me a kiss. For me that's really uncomfortable. (Pia)

When Grandma takes me in her arms, it's nice at first, but then she doesn't stop hugging. I can't get any air and become quite irritated. I'd love to just run away from there. (Paul)

In 6th Grade, Till persuaded me to go with him to the supermarket to steal. I didn't want to at all. Till says it is our secret, if I tell, something bad will happen. I feel terrible whenever I think about it. (Lance)

If something doesn't feel good to you, you always have the right to say NO! Even if others are offended. Someone who likes you will accept your "No!" and not pressure you.

Saying No Is Sometimes Quite Difficult!

It sounds so simple: say no when something doesn't feel good.

Laura, Serafina's cousin, has experienced what it was like to not know whether to say yes or no.

Once Uncle Linus came to visit. He's the brother of Laura's mother.

Uncle Linus showed Laura how to surf the Internet. He showed her where to find the best games and how to download her favorite songs from the web. They sat very close to each other at the computer. Laura had a nice warm feeling in her stomach. Uncle Linus laid his arm around Laura and began to caress her.

He stuck a hand under her sweater. Suddenly, she didn't feel so good anymore. Laura began to feel uncomfortable. She would have liked to say "Stop it!" But it was strange for her because Uncle Linus is really nice.

Laura became very rigid. She had hoped that Uncle Linus himself would realize that he should stop. But he kept on caressing her.

He stroked Laura's legs and slipped his hand under her waistband. Laura felt that she didn't want what Uncle Linus was doing to her. But somehow she had missed the opportunity to say no. Uncle Linus's voice became quite gruff and he looked so strange. Very different than usual. Then he kissed her on the ear and told her that she shouldn't tell anyone how fond Uncle Linus was of her, and that her mother would certainly be very unhappy if she heard. And that then she wouldn't love Laura anymore.

"It's our big se-cret!" Uncle Linus said.

From then on, Laura tried to avoid Uncle Linus.

"What's going on with my little princess?" he asked. "You don't love your uncle anymore."

He kept trying to be alone again with Laura and to caress her.

Laura felt that this secret was like a heavy black cloud that she brought with her everywhere.

At some point she could no longer bear it and told Serafina the whole story. Luckily, Serafina knew that one should never keep a bad secret. They went together to Laura's mother and told her everything.

Laura's mother was very angry with her brother but she loved Laura just as much as before. She went with her to a counseling center. There was a nice woman there who helped Laura to understand that she is no way to blame for this whole matter with Uncle Linus. Even if she didn't succeed in saying "No!" and "Stop it!" to him, like she wanted.

No!

No!

No!

Important!

You always have the right to say **No!**

But even if you don't manage to say **No!**, you are still not to blame.

Nobody has to keep a terrible secret to him- or herself.

Whoever makes you keep such a secret does not really mean well for you.

Bad secrets are hard to keep for anyone. Especially for a child. Tell someone you trust what's on your mind. If you don't dare go to someone around you, then you can call a counseling center.

You can find addresses and telephone numbers at the end of this book.

Children Have Rights

Children do not only have the right to say **No!** when they don't like something.

The UN Convention on the Rights of the Child has put together a list of rights which should apply to children all over the world:

 All children have the same rights. No child should be at a disadvantage because of his or her skin color, language, or religion, or because of being a girl or a boy.

 Children have the right to live as healthily as possible.

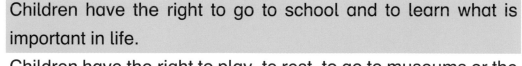 Children have the right to go to school and to learn what is important in life.

 Children have the right to play, to rest, to go to museums or the movies, or, for example, to act in plays themselves.

5. Children have the right to inform themselves, to say what they think, and to be heard.

6. Children have the right to be educated without the threat of violence.

 **7.** Children have the right to be protected, especially if there is war in their country and/or they are refugees.

 8. Children have the right to be protected from harmful work, exploitation, and abuse.

 9. Children have the right to live with their parents, or, if they don't live together, to visit regularly with their mother or father.

 **10.** Children with disabilities have the right to receive help and to play and learn together with other children.learn together with other children.

Equal Rights for Girls and Boys. Yes, Of Course!

"No child should be disadvantaged because of being a girl or a boy. That's stated in the Rights of the Child. But isn't that already clear?" Paul wonders. Jasper, Robert, and Lea nod.

"Then why do I always have to help wash the dishes when my brother doesn't?" asks Hannah.

"Your brother is still little," Hazima answers. "When he's a little older, he'll have to help too, otherwise it's not fair."

"Washing is a woman's job," Radley smirks.

"Do you live under a rock?" counters Kai. "Maybe that was once the case, when my grandfather was a little boy. And even he helps my grandmother with the house-work."

Actually, it really is clear: Girls and boys, men and women—all have the same rights and obligations.

Children are protected by the basic rights embodied by the Constitution, and the Equal Protection Clause of the Fourteenth Amendment of the United States.

Nevertheless, there is still some un-fairness. "For example, when a woman earns less than a man even though they do the same job," says Lea.

"Exactly!" Kai frowns. "Or when someone says: 'In our class there are 25 schoolboys.'"

"Why? It's true!" Luis shrugs his shoulders.

"It should be schoolboys and schoolgirls," says Kai. "Otherwise it feels like there aren't any of us. Us girls, I mean."

"Oh." Luis nods. "I see."

"My friend Sevim is from Turkey. She must always wear a headscarf and not go out alone. Her brother can, though, even though he's younger. That's why others often make fun of her. Also, her father wants her to eventually marry a man that he picks for her. We don't see that a lot in the United States these days," Sam reflects. Sevim comes from another country and from a different culture where this is the norm, though.

The US Constitution states that no one should be disadvantaged or favored because of his or her sex, orientation, ethnicity, race, language, homeland of origin, faith, or religious or political views.

For example, this means Sevim and her family have the right to wear headscarves—there is no reason to laugh at them or prohibit it.

When do girls feel at a disadvantage, and when do boys? It can be fascinating to talk about in class.

29

Firewoman, Pediatric Nurse— What Do I Want to Be?

Stella wants to be a firefighter.

"Women can't do that," says Jasper.

"Sure they can," Lea says, "Women can do it just as well as men." Lea wants to be lawyer like her mother and Jasper wants to be a concert violinist.

Sam would like to be an actress and Luis wants to be a ballet dancer. "Cool," says Lance. "Then I can sew your costumes. I mostly want to be either a tailor or a fashion designer."

Radley wants to be an astronaut and his friend Daniel wants to be a space engineer. Kurt wants to be a chef. And one heck of one!

Toby and Robert want to work at the hospital, Toby as a doctor and Robert as a pediatric nurse. Serafina wants to become a racecar driver. With bright red super-fast car.

Kai dreams of becoming the first female president. Pauline wants to work at the bank, but Regina can't understand why.

"I thought you wanted to be a writer and have me draw the pictures for your stories. Working at the bank is more Hannah's style." But Hannah wants to open a shop. Just like David.

Paul and Hazima want to be tour guides. Dale dreams of a career as an architect and Uriel would like to be a carpenter. "And what about your poems?" asks Bernard, who wants to work in his father's bookstore.

Pia and Lisa want to be veterinarians. "Great, then you can take turns coming to me when I have my horseback-riding academy," Nicki laughs.

Full Coverage—
Older Siblings in Puberty

Last year Jan, Jasper's older brother, was not much different from Jasper. Of course, Jan has always been bigger than Jasper. But he has the same dark hair and the same brown eyes as his brother. For some time now, however, Jan has begun to change more and more.

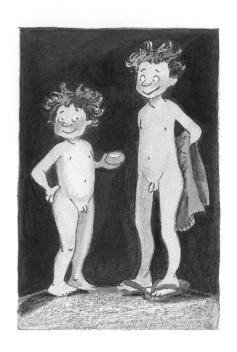

His shoulders are wider. Suddenly he's getting pimples. A delicate dark fluff is growing on his upper lip. His penis is getting bigger, and dark, curly hairs have started to grow around it. Jasper finds Jan's voice most interesting. Sometimes it is deep and then, suddenly, it gets high again. From his dad, Jasper knows this is referred to as one's voice breaking. If he laughs about it, Jan gets angry.

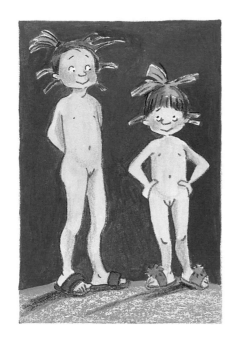

Stella's older sister, Nora, is in the same grade as Jan. And she's changing, too. If Stella sees her sister showering, she is pretty amazed. Nora now has breasts. "Not so small, either," Stella thinks. Nora's hips are wider and she's growing red pubic hair. She also gets pimples every now and then. When that happens, she doesn't want to go to school at all. Once a month, Nora gets her period. A bit of blood flows from her vagina and sometimes it also hurts her stomach. Stella's mother gives her a heating pad.

I don't get it!

Oh my God, I am so ugly!!!!

Puberty—Not Everything Is on the Outside

Jan and Nora are not only changing on the outside. Even a year ago, Jan sometimes played with Jasper. Together they built stuff with Legos or did experiments with the chemistry kit. Now Jan no longer wants to. He no longer wants to do almost anything, Jasper finds. Jan is constantly in a bad mood and hangs around in his room. If a family member wants to do something with him, he finds it "so embarrassing!" His mood only gets better if he makes plans with his friends. Then he spends hours in the bathroom. When he comes out, he smells like a whole cologne store. Before, Jasper knows full well, Jan was just as reluctant to wash up as Jasper.

"I'll never be that way!" mutters Jasper.
"Just wait," says Mama. "At some point you'll hit puberty too."
"No way!" thinks Jasper.

Lately Nora loves reading romance novels. She talks on the phone for hours with her friends, finds everything "Sweeeet!" and is permanently giggling.

Any time she is extremely unhappy about something, she stays in her room and listens to very sad songs. This gets on Stella's nerves. She hardly knows Nora anymore. Stella doesn't understand why her sister constantly complains about herself. Before, Nora was a star in the Judo Club; now, she often skips training sessions. Instead, she stands in front of the mirror and whines about her pimples or her legs (too thick), and her breasts, which she finds too small.

"Complete nonsense!" thinks Stella, but no one asks her what she thinks.

Jan and Nora are going through puberty. This period in which people's body and spirit change is not so easy. A person is a still somewhat a child and already somewhat an adult. One moment you're down in the dumps and in the next moment you can feel like a million bucks.

All people must go through it at some point—even Jasper and Stella.

And What's Up With Love?

Jan and Nora are in love. That is to say, Jan is in love with Nora. If he sees her, he turns as red as a tomato. And he doesn't dare say anything because he's afraid that his voice will get that strange squeak.

Nora is in love with Fred from class 9C. If she sees him, she gets very weak in the knees. Recently, Nora kissed Fred at a birthday party. Only very gently on the lips. Later, Fred touched Nora's tongue with his tongue. Nora got goosebumps all over her body and her belly felt quite hot. Nora would've liked to continue kissing, but then her dad came and picked her up. Too bad!

If couples don't want to have children, they use contraceptives. The man pulls the condom over his penis. It captures the semen (which contains sperm) before it can enter the vagina.

Jan has a terrible heartache thanks to Nora. His mother says it will pass. But Jan can't imagine that, not for the life of him. He will always love Nora, he's quite sure of this.

Toby also has a big sister. Sabrina is already grown up. At least 20 years old. She has been in love with Marco for a long time. The two of them live in a small apartment, very close to Toby and his parents.

"Marco is a great guy," Toby thinks. When he grows up, he wants to drive as nice a motor scooter as Marco. Secretly, he imagines himself racing around with Serafina riding on the back.

Sabrina and Marco kiss often. "All the time," thinks Toby.

And they also sleep together. Sabrina told Toby so.

They snuggle together for a long time. They kiss each other all over their bodies. Behind the ears, on the neck, on the chest and stomach, even on the bum and between the legs. Sabrina's vagina becomes moist and warm and Marco's penis gets very stiff. Marco then pushes his penis into Sabrina's vagina. Always in and out. That feels great for both of them. When the feeling is nicest, Marco's penis sprays semen into Sabrina's vagina.

"That's how you get babies," Toby said.

"You guessed it, little brother," Sabrina said, and tousled Toby's hair.

Women take birth control pills to prevent the fertilization of an egg.

The IUD is inserted into the uterus. It prevents a fertilized egg from attaching to the uterine lining.

The diaphragm is a rubber cap that is slipped around the cervix. That's how it keeps sperm from entering the uterus.

Contraceptive foam caps are inserted into the vagina. The foam forms a barrier against the semen.

Help! I'm Going to Be an Uncle!

Toby already knew: if two people sleep together without using contraceptives, they can make a baby, and now Sabrina is pregnant. It's plain to see. Toby will become an uncle.

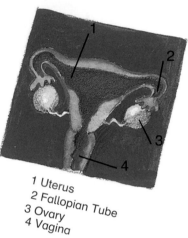

1 Uterus
2 Fallopian Tube
3 Ovary
4 Vagina

At some point, Sabrina stopped getting her period. Normally, an adult woman gets her period once a month. Once the egg has journeyed from the ovary to the uterus, it is then cast out. Then some blood flows from the vagina.

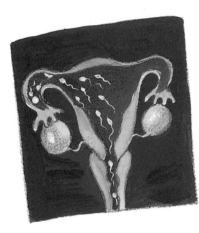

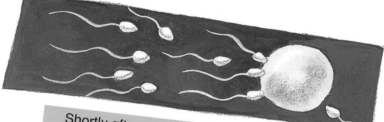

Shortly after the egg has left the ovary, it can be fertilized.
When the sperm enter into the vagina, they make their way to the egg.

The sperm organize a kind of swimming competition, because only the first sperm will be taken by the egg. When the sperm cell has fused with the egg cell, the egg is fertilized. Sometimes the fertilized egg cell divides itself at an early stage. Then you get twins.

After the fertilization, the egg cell begins to divide itself and the new egg cells also keep dividing themselves. This mass of cells moves slowly into the uterus.

After a month, the baby (at this stage, it is called a fetus) is about two millimeters long.

The baby grows and grows. It feeds through the umbilical cord. The womb also keeps getting bigger and bigger. But after nine months it will be too small for the baby. It is time for birth. During this, the baby pushes headfirst through the vagina, which can stretch wide enough for the baby to fit through.

Finally the time came. Toby held his little niece in his arms. "What should we call your little niece, Uncle Toby?" Marco asked.

"Serafina!" Toby said.

So, Here's How It Goes!

Sabrina and Marco have known each other for a long time. They went to school together. Many years ago, they were both together in Class 4B, with the same teacher as Toby, Stella, Nicki, Serafina, Radley, and all the rest. The boys sat by the window and the girls sat on the other side, by the door.

Sabrina and Marco on the first day of school.

At the time, Sabrina found Marco dumb. And Marco found Sabrina and the other girls all totally stupid.

When Sabrina was 15, she was going out with Hartmut. She thought he was totally sweet. Back then, Marco went around with a motorcycle helmet, even though he didn't even have a moped. Sabrina thought that was silly.

Sabrina and Marco only fell in love after finishing school. They met each other again at a quarry pond. Since then, they've been inseparable.

Sabrina
+
Marco

41

You Can Always Fall In Love

Horice and Ethel Bamberg met each other three years ago at Lake Ariel.

Bea and Jo got back together recently. Before they were on a break for three months.

Lu and Ricardo want to have many children together. At least four.

Theo and Sabine are quite newly smitten.

For Mrs. Martins, Karl is the best.

Susie and Mike want to go to Italy together.

Leon never wants to
let Ralph go again.

Mrs. Gold and Mr. Fish
are newly in love.

Manny confessed to Helga
by text yesterday how
much he loves her.

Teddy and Monster
like to cuddle.

Mrs. and Mr. Rübel fell in
love 52 years ago. "Oh,
yes!" says Mr. Rübel.

Tim and Lumpi fall in love every spring.

Ms. Mayer and Mr. Hook met
online, even though they are
teachers at the same school.

Dagmar Geisler, who grew up in Hesse, lives in Franconian Switzerland (Bavaria) and has been writing with growing enthusiasm for 15 years for children and young people. As a trained illustrator, she also takes care of the design and finds great joy in this combination. She enjoys drawing cartoons for adults and for this reason a touch of humor certainly appears throughout her work.

Resources

Administration for Children and Families
U.S. Department of Health & Human Services
330 C Street SW Washington, DC 20201
www.acf.hhs.gov

Advocates for Youth
Advocates for Youth
1325 G Street NW, Suite 980
Washington, DC 20005
www.advocatesforyouth.org

Amaze.org
AMAZE.org
c/o Advocates for Youth
1325 G Street NW, Suite 980
Washington, DC 20005
www.amaze.org

American Academy of Pediatrics (AAP)
American Academy of Pediatrics
National Headquarters
345 Park Boulevard
Itasca, IL 60143
www.aap.org

American Red Cross
American Red Cross National Headquarters
431 18th Street NW
Washington, DC 20006
www.redcross.org

American Sexual Health Association
ASHA
P.O. Box 13287
Research Triangle Park, NC 22709
www.ashasexualhealth.org

Centers for Disease Control and Prevention (CDC)
Centers for Disease Control and Prevention
1600 Clifton Road
Atlanta, GA 30333
www.cdc.gov

Head Start
U.S. Department of Health & Human Services
330 C Street SW
Washington, DC 20201
www.acf.hhs.gov/ohs

HealthyChildren.org
American Academy of Pediatrics
National Headquarters
345 Park Boulevard
Itasca, IL 60143
www.healthychildren.org

National Association for Family Child Care (NAFCC)
NAFCC
1743 West Alexander Street #201
Salt Lake City, UT 84119
www.nafcc.org

National Association for the Education of Young Children
NAEYC Headquarters
1313 L Street NW, Suite 500
Washington, DC 20005-4101
www.naeyc.org

National Center for Families Learning
National Center for Families Learning
325 W Main Street #300
Louisville, KY 40202
www.familieslearning.org

National Center for Parent, Family, and

Community Engagement
U.S. Department of Health & Human
Services
330 C Street SW
Washington, DC 20201
childcareta.acf.hhs.gov

National Institutes of Health (NIH)
National Institutes of Health
9000 Rockville Pike
Bethesda, MD 20892
www.nih.gov

Parents as Teachers
Parents as Teachers National Center,
Inc.
2228 Ball Drive
St. Louis, MO 63146
www.parentsasteachers.org

Planned Parenthood
Planned Parenthood Federation
of America
123 William Street, 10th Floor
New York, NY 10038
www.plannedparenthood.org

Unhushed
Unhushed
P.O. Box 92033
Austin, TX 78709
www.unhushed.org

Index

Baby 39
Basic Law 28, 29
Being in Love 11–13, 36, 41–43
Birth 39
Birth Control Pills 37
Breasts 33

Cervix 37
Children's Rights 26–28
Coil 37
Condom 36
Contraceptive Foam 37
Counselling Centers 24, 25
Cuddling 17

Diaphragm 37

Egg 37, 38
Egg Cells 38, 39

Fallopian Tubes 38
Fertilization 37–39
Fetus 39

Gender Equality 28, 29

Heartache 36
Holding Hands 15, 16

Kissing 36, 37

Ovary 38

Penis 32, 36, 37
Period 33, 38
Pimples 32, 33
Pregnancy 38, 39
Protection 36, 37
Puberty 32–35
Pubic hair 32, 33

Rights see Children's Rights

Saying no 18, 19, 21–24
Saying yes 18, 19
Scuffling 14–16
Secret 19–21, 23–25
Semen 36, 37
Seminal fluid 36
Sperm 37, 38

Twins 38

Umbilical Cord 39
UN Convention on the
Rights of the Child 26
Uterus 37–39

Vagina 33, 36–39
Voice Breaking 32